Our Solar System
C O N C E P T   S C I E N C E

by Colin Walker • Pictures by Philip Webb

A solar system is a sun
and everything that moves around it.
Planets, comets, asteroids, moons,
and meteors are all part
of a solar system.

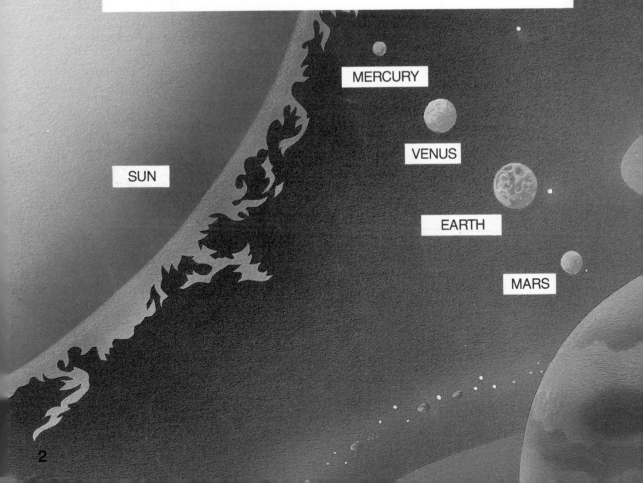

MERCURY

VENUS

SUN

EARTH

MARS

PLUTO

URANUS

NEPTUNE

SATURN

PITER

3

Our Sun is a star.
It is the center of our solar system.

SUN

PLUTO

NEPTUNE

SATURN

URANUS

JUPITER

In our solar system
there are nine planets.
Each planet moves around, or orbits,
the Sun.

MERCURY

VENUS

SUN

EARTH

MARS

Mercury is the closest planet to the Sun.
As it spins, it is very hot on the side
facing the Sun and very cold on the side
away from the Sun.

Venus shines brightly in the sky.
It is about the same size as Earth.
Venus is a very hot planet.
It is surrounded by clouds.

Earth is a planet.
It spins round and round.
The spinning Earth orbits the Sun.
Our moon orbits Earth.

Mars is about half the size of Earth.
Mars often looks red.
It has huge volcanoes,
canyons, and rock deserts.

Jupiter is the biggest planet
in our solar system.
Jupiter has many moons
orbiting its cloudy surface.

Saturn is the second largest planet.
It has bright rings around it.
These rings may be made of ice
and perhaps some rock.

Uranus and Neptune are about
the same size.
They are both very cold
and are made mainly of gases.

Pluto is the smallest planet.
It is often furthest away from the Sun.
Pluto is a cold, dark planet.

QUIZ

Find out what you know.

What makes up a solar system?

What is at the center of our solar system?

What word, meaning "travels around" finishes this sentence? Each planet _____ the Sun.

How many planets are there in our solar system?

Try these activities:

1. With a partner, make a chart about the planets. Use library books to learn more about the planets which interest you the most. Share your chart with the rest of the class.

PLANETS IN OUR SOLAR SYSTEM

Name	Temperature	Size	Moons

2. Imagine that you are an astronaut. On a trip into outer space, you just discovered a planet. What color is it? Does it have moons or rings around it? Is it cold or hot? Does its surface have rocks and mountains, or is it flat? Draw a picture of the planet to share with your friends.